THE C ...arp)

Zak Wakeman is a movie director in Hollywood. He is making a movie with the famous star, Natalie Nevons. Nathan is in the movie, too. He does Natalie's stunts because they are dangerous. Zak does not think Natalie can do stunts, but she thinks she can.

Tonight, Zak is having a big party. Natalie and Nathan are there . . . and so is The Cat! The Cat steals things from people with lots of money. He is going to steal from Zak Wakeman. The police are trying to find him.

Who is The Cat?

Can Natalie and Nathan stop him?

OXFORD BOOKWORMS LIBRARY

Crime & Mystery

The Cat

Starter (250 headwords)

JOHN ESCOTT

The Cat

Illustrated by
Camille Corbetto

OXFORD UNIVERSITY PRESS

OXFORD
UNIVERSITY PRESS

Great Clarendon Street, Oxford, OX2 6DP, United Kingdom

Oxford University Press is a department of the University of Oxford.
It furthers the University's objective of excellence in research, scholarship,
and education by publishing worldwide. Oxford is a registered trade
mark of Oxford University Press in the UK and in certain other countries

ISBN: 978 0 19 478609 6

A complete recording of this Bookworms edition of
The Cat is available in a CD pack ISBN: 978 0 19 478598 3

Printed in China

Word count (main text): 1,292 words

For more information on the Oxford Bookworms Library,
visit www.oup.com/elt/gradedreaders

ACKNOWLEDGEMENTS

Illustrations by: Camille Corbetto, colagene.com

CONTENTS

THE CAT

The year is 1935. The place is Hollywood.

The Los Angeles newspapers call him The Cat.
He steals at night.

Tonight he is at a house in the Hollywood Hills. The
people in the house are having a party. They cannot see
or hear The Cat. He is on the roof.

'I need to get to that window,' he thinks.

Minutes later, he is making a hole in the window.

The Cat opens the window and gets into a bedroom. He listens, but everything is quiet in the room. The only noise is the party.

'Now I must find the jewels!' he thinks.

It only takes him a minute or two to find them.

'I can get hundreds of dollars for these!' he thinks.

Moving quickly, he puts them into his bag and leaves.

Next day, at Starshine Studios, Zak Wakeman is making a movie.

The star of the movie is Natalie Nevons. She begins to act.

'OK, Natalie,' Zak says. 'Act very afraid. You want to get out of the building. You look up . . . you can't see Brad. But Brad, you *can* see Natalie, and you're waiting for her . . .'

'OK!' says Zak. 'Now bring on the stand-ins.'

The stand-ins are Nathan and Bud. They do all the dangerous things in the movie, all the stunts. Nathan is Natalie's stand-in, and Bud is Brad Poole's stand-in.

'Good luck, Nathan!' says Natalie.

'Thanks, Miss Nevons,' says Nathan.

Brad says nothing to Bud.

'OK!' calls Zak. 'Begin to climb up the building, Nathan.'

The two stand-ins begin to act. Nathan climbs out of the window and up onto the roof of the building.

Bud is waiting for him.

'At first you don't see Bud, Nathan!' calls Zak. 'Now you do! And Bud, you try to stop Nathan, but he gets away.'

Nathan quickly gets away from Bud and runs across the roof of the building.

Bud runs after him.

Natalie Nevons is watching them.

'I can do that,' she thinks. 'Nathan is very good, but I don't need a stand-in.'

'OK, everybody,' calls Zak. 'We are beginning again in twenty minutes.'

'I like your hair, Nathan!' says Bud, laughing. 'It's very nice. You're very pretty!'

Nathan is angry, but he says nothing. He does not like Bud.

Natalie goes to speak to Zak.

'What's wrong, Natalie?' Zak asks.

'Mr Wakeman, please can I do some of my stunts?' asks Natalie. 'I don't always need a stand-in.'

'Sorry, Natalie,' says Zak. 'The stunts are too dangerous.'

'Why do you want to do your stunts, Natalie?' Brad Poole asks her. 'I'm happy to leave the dangerous acting to Bud.'

'Are you coming to my party tonight, Natalie?' Zak asks.
'It begins at eight o'clock.'

'Yes, Mr Wakeman,' says Natalie.

'Me, too,' says Brad.

Zak goes to speak to Nathan.

'I can give you twenty dollars to park the cars at my
party tonight, Nathan,' he says. 'Do you want to do it?'

'Yes, please, Mr Wakeman,' says Nathan.

That night, Natalie Nevons arrives at Zak Wakeman's house in the Hollywood Hills.

'Hi, Miss Nevons,' says Nathan.

'Hi, Nathan,' says Natalie. 'Are you working here tonight?'

'Yes,' says Nathan. 'I'm helping to park the cars.'

'Why?' asks Natalie.

'Because I need the money,' Nathan tells her.

The Cat is out again. This time, he is going to steal from Zak Wakeman's house. He leaves his car near the trees and waits. Quickly, he runs across to the building and begins to climb.

Nathan does not see The Cat. He is watching Natalie Nevons go into the house.

'There are lots of movie stars here tonight,' he thinks. 'But Miss Nevons is the most beautiful.'

After some time, Nathan goes to look at the swimming pool.

A minute later, he sees Natalie Nevons. She is coming out of the house. She has two drinks.

'I have a drink for you, Nathan,' she says.

'Oh – thanks, Miss Nevons,' says Nathan.

'You're a good stand-in, Nathan,' she says. 'But I want to do some of my stunts in the movie. Mr Wakeman says "no" but I . . .'

Suddenly, she sees someone running to the trees.

'Look!' she says. 'Who's that?'

'It's The Cat!' says Nathan. 'Remember him from the newspaper? He's going to that car!'

'Quick!' says Natalie. 'Let's get my car!'

'Do you want me to drive?' Nathan asks. 'I can drive really fast.'

'No!' Natalie tells him. 'I'm driving!'

Natalie drives fast and it is a dangerous road.

'Be careful, Miss Nevons,' says Nathan. 'You have a movie to finish, remember!'

'It's OK, I'm a good driver,' she says. She smiles. 'And you can call me Natalie.'

Nathan smiles, too. 'OK,' he says.

'We're getting near to him!' says Natalie.

'Yes, but look! There's a train coming!' says Nathan.

Natalie looks quickly. 'It's OK!' she says. 'It's not going to hit us.'

The train is moving fast.

'We aren't going to do it!' says Nathan.

'Yes, we *are*!' Natalie tells him.

'Wow! That was close!' says Nathan.

Natalie laughs, and says nothing.

Suddenly, two policemen see Natalie's car.

'Look at them!' says one policeman. 'How fast are they going, Joe?'

'Too fast, Sam,' says Joe. 'Let's stop them.'

'It's not going to be easy,' says Sam, 'but let's go!'

Suddenly, Nathan sees the police car.

'Er, Natalie,' he says.

'What is it?' she asks.

'There's a police car behind us,' says Nathan. 'It wants us to stop.'

'I'm not stopping,' she says. 'It's OK, we can tell them everything later. First we have to stop The Cat.'

Suddenly, The Cat sees the police car, too.

'Oh, no!' he says. 'I need to get out of this car.'

He stops his car and runs.

Soon after, Natalie and Nathan are jumping from Natalie's car. The Cat looks back and sees them. 'They're stopping, too,' he thinks. 'So, who can run the fastest?'

Minutes later, the police car stops near Natalie's car. The two policemen jump out, and look for Natalie and Nathan.

'Where are they, Sam?' asks Joe.

'I don't know,' says Sam. 'I can't see them. There are too many people.'

'There he is!' says Natalie. 'There's The Cat!'

'He's running to that building,' says Nathan.

'Let's go!' says Natalie, and she runs after The Cat.

Nathan runs after her. 'He's going up to the roof!' he says.

And the three of them begin to climb up to the roof of the building.

Suddenly, The Cat throws his bag at Natalie. She does not
see it, but Nathan does.

'Natalie, the bag!' he calls.

The bag does not hit Natalie, but it hits Nathan.

'Nathan, are you all right?' calls Natalie.

'I'm OK,' says Nathan.

The Cat and Natalie run across the roof of the building.
Then, The Cat jumps from one building to the next.

Natalie watches him. 'Can I do that?' she thinks.

Natalie jumps.

Nathan sees her. 'Wow! Look at her!' he thinks.

The Cat sees her, too. 'How can I get away from her?'
he thinks.

He *cannot* get away from her.

'Got you!' says Natalie, and she jumps on him. 'So who are you?'

She takes off The Cat's mask. 'You!' she says.

'It's Bud!' says Nathan.

The policemen arrive and look from Natalie to Bud and back again.

'It's the movie star, Natalie Nevons!' says Joe.

'Yes!' says Sam. 'And The Cat!'

The next day, Nathan and Natalie tell Zak their story. 'Bud is The Cat?' he asks.

'That's right,' says Natalie.

'And you want to be Brad's new stand-in?' Zak says to Nathan. 'OK, but we need a new stand-in for Natalie. Who can do her stunts?'

'Natalie doesn't need a stand-in!' says Nathan, laughing. '*She* can do her stunts!'

GLOSSARY

act *(v)* be somebody in a movie *(n)* **acting**

climb *(v)* go up or down using your hands and feet

dangerous something that can hurt or kill you

director someone who makes movies

dollars money used in America

jewels expensive and beautiful stones

jump *(v)* move both your feet quickly off the ground

movie you go to the cinema to watch a movie

newspaper you read about the things that happen every
  day in a newspaper

park *(v)* put or leave a car in a place

party *(n)* people or friends meet to have fun at a party

place *(n)* where something happens

policeman a policeman stops people doing bad things

roof the top of a building

stand-in *(n)* a stand-in does the stunts in a movie

star *(n)* the most important actor in a movie

steal *(v)* take something that is not yours

story something you read in a book; *The Cat* is a story

stunt something dangerous and exciting in a movie

throw *(v)* move your arm and hand quickly to send
  something through the air

try have a go at doing something

twenty 20

The Cat

ACTIVITIES

Before Reading

1 **Read the back cover of the book and answer these questions.**

1 What does The Cat do?
2 What is Natalie?
3 What does Nathan do?
4 Where is Zak's home?

2 **Look at the picture on page 1 and answer these questions.**

1 Where do you think this story happens?
   a ☐ Italy
   b ☐ China
   c ☐ America
   d ☐ Australia

2 When do you think this story happens?
   a ☐ now
   b ☐ 1930s
   c ☐ 2020

While Reading

1 Read pages 1–5 and answer these questions.

  1 What does The Cat steal from the bedroom?

  2 Who is making a movie at Starshine Studios?

  3 Who is the star of the movie?

  4 Who is Brad Poole's stand-in?

2 Read pages 6–8. Who says or thinks these words?

  1 'Nathan is very good, but I don't need a stand-in.'

  2 'OK, everybody. We are beginning again in twenty minutes.'

  3 'You're very pretty!'

  4 'Sorry, Natalie. The stunts are too dangerous.'

  5 'I'm happy to leave the dangerous acting to Bud.'

3 Read pages 9–12 and answer these questions.

  1 What does Zak ask Nathan to do?

  2 How much is Zak paying Nathan?

  3 Where does The Cat park his car?

  4 What does Natalie want to do?

4 Read pages 13–18. Are these sentences true (T) or false (F)?

	T	F
1 Natalie sees someone running to the trees.	☐	☐
2 Nathan drives Natalie's car.	☐	☐
3 A train hits Natalie's car.	☐	☐
4 Two policemen see Natalie's car.	☐	☐
5 Natalie stops the car to talk to the policemen.	☐	☐
6 The Cat sees the police car.	☐	☐

5 Read pages 19–22 and answer these questions.

1 Why can't the policemen see Nathan and Natalie?
2 Where is The Cat running to?
3 What does The Cat throw?
4 Who does it hit?
5 Where does The Cat jump to?

6 Before reading pages 23–24, can you guess what happens?

	Yes	No
1 The Cat gets away.	☐	☐
2 The Cat falls and hits his head.	☐	☐
3 Natalie jumps on The Cat.	☐	☐
4 Brad Poole is The Cat.	☐	☐
5 Bud is The Cat.	☐	☐
6 Zak says Natalie can do stunts.	☐	☐

Now read pages 23–24 to find out the answers.

After Reading

1 **Put these sentences in the correct order. Number them 1–10.**

a ☐ The policemen lose Natalie and Nathan.

b ☐ Nathan climbs out of the window and up on to the roof.

c ☐ Natalie sees The Cat running to the trees.

d ☐ The Cat throws something.

e ☐ Zak says Natalie cannot do stunts.

f ☐ Natalie pulls off The Cat's mask.

g ☐ Nathan sees a train coming.

h ☐ The Cat finds the jewels.

i ☐ Nathan is Brad's new stand-in.

j ☐ Nathan parks cars at Zak's party.

2 **Use these words to join the sentences together.**

but   from   into   at   and

1 He is going to steal. A house in the Hollywood Hills.

2 Nathan gets away from Bud. Runs across the roof of the building.

3 'You try to stop her. She gets away.'

4 Natalie Nevons arrives. Zak's house.

5 He is watching Natalie Nevons go. The house.

3 Look at the pictures and answer these questions.

a Whose hand is this?
b What is he or she doing?

a Who is Natalie talking to?
b What is she asking him?

a What are Nathan and
  Natalie doing?
b Why is Nathan afraid?

a What are they doing?
b What happens next?

ABOUT THE AUTHOR

John Escott worked in business before becoming a writer. He has written many books for readers of all ages, but enjoys writing crime and mystery thrillers most of all. He was born in Somerset, in the west of England, but now lives in Bournemouth, on the south coast.

He has written or retold more than twenty stories for the Oxford Bookworms Library. His original stories include The Girl with Green Eyes (Starter), Dead Man's Money (Starter), Star Reporter (Starter), Girl on a Motorcycle (Starter), Goodbye, Mr Hollywood (Stage 1), and Sister Love and Other Crime Stories (Stage 1).

OXFORD BOOKWORMS LIBRARY

Classics • Crime & Mystery • Factfiles • Fantasy & Horror
Human Interest • Playscripts • Thriller & Adventure
True Stories • World Stories

The OXFORD BOOKWORMS LIBRARY provides enjoyable reading in English, with a wide range of classic and modern fiction, non-fiction, and plays. It includes original and adapted texts in seven carefully graded language stages, which take learners from beginner to advanced level. An overview is given on the next pages.

All Stage 1 titles are available as audio recordings, as well as over eighty other titles from Starter to Stage 6. All Starters and many titles at Stages 1 to 4 are specially recommended for younger learners. Every Bookworm is illustrated, and Starters and Factfiles have full-colour illustrations.

The OXFORD BOOKWORMS LIBRARY also offers extensive support. Each book contains an introduction to the story, notes about the author, a glossary, and activities. Additional resources include tests and worksheets, and answers for these and for the activities in the books. There is advice on running a class library, using audio recordings, and the many ways of using Oxford Bookworms in reading programmes. Resource materials are available on the website <www.oup.com/elt/gradedreaders>.

The Oxford Bookworms Collection is a series for advanced learners. It consists of volumes of short stories by well-known authors, both classic and modern. Texts are not abridged or adapted in any way, but carefully selected to be accessible to the advanced student.

You can find details and a full list of titles in the *Oxford Bookworms Library Catalogue* and *Oxford English Language Teaching Catalogues*, and on the website <www.oup.com/elt/gradedreaders>.

THE OXFORD BOOKWORMS LIBRARY
GRADING AND SAMPLE EXTRACTS

STARTER • 250 HEADWORDS

present simple – present continuous – imperative –
can/cannot, *must* – *going to* (future) – simple gerunds ...

Her phone is ringing – but where is it?

Sally gets out of bed and looks in her bag. No phone. She looks under the bed. No phone. Then she looks behind the door. There is her phone. Sally picks up her phone and answers it. *Sally's Phone*

STAGE 1 • 400 HEADWORDS

... past simple – coordination with *and*, *but*, *or* –
subordination with *before*, *after*, *when*, *because*, *so* ...

I knew him in Persia. He was a famous builder and I worked with him there. For a time I was his friend, but not for long. When he came to Paris, I came after him – I wanted to watch him. He was a very clever, very dangerous man. *The Phantom of the Opera*

STAGE 2 • 700 HEADWORDS

... present perfect – *will* (future) – (*don't*) *have to*, *must not*, *could* –
comparison of adjectives – simple *if* clauses – past continuous –
tag questions – *ask/tell* + infinitive ...

While I was writing these words in my diary, I decided what to do. I must try to escape. I shall try to get down the wall outside. The window is high above the ground, but I have to try. I shall take some of the gold with me – if I escape, perhaps it will be helpful later. *Dracula*

… should, may – present perfect continuous – *used to* – past perfect –
causative – relative clauses – indirect statements …

Of course, it was most important that no one should see
Colin, Mary, or Dickon entering the secret garden. So Colin
gave orders to the gardeners that they must all keep away
from that part of the garden in future. ***The Secret Garden***

STAGE 4 • 1400 HEADWORDS

… past perfect continuous – passive (simple forms) –
would conditional clauses indirect questions –
relatives with *where/when* – gerunds after prepositions/phrases …

I was glad. Now Hyde could not show his face to the world
again. If he did, every honest man in London would be
proud to report him to the police. ***Dr Jekyll and Mr Hyde***

STAGE 5 • 1800 HEADWORDS

… future continuous – future perfect –
passive (modals, continuous forms) –
would have conditional clauses – modals + perfect infinitive …

If he had spoken Estella's name, I would have hit him. I was
so angry with him, and so depressed about my future, that I
could not eat the breakfast. Instead I went straight to the old
house. ***Great Expectations***

STAGE 6 • 2500 HEADWORDS

… passive (infinitives, gerunds) – advanced modal meanings –
clauses of concession, condition

When I stepped up to the piano, I was confident. It was as if
I knew that the prodigy side of me really did exist. And when I
started to play, I was so caught up in how lovely I looked that I
didn't worry how I would sound. ***The Joy Luck Club***

BOOKWORMS · CRIME & MYSTERY · STARTER
Dead Man's Money
JOHN ESCOTT

When Cal Dexter rents one of the Blue Lake Cabins, he finds $3000 _ under the floor! He doesn't know it, but it is the money from a bank robbery. A dead man's money.

'Do I take it to the police?' he thinks.

But three more people want the money, and two of them are dangerous.

BOOKWORMS · CRIME & MYSTERY · STARTER
The Mystery of Manor Hall
JANE CAMMOCK

Manor Hall is an old dark house with a mystery. Nobody can go into the music room. But one night Tom and Milly hear something. The noise is coming from the music room.

Tom and Milly open the door. Someone in the music room is singing. Tom and Milly are afraid, but they can't move.

Can Tom and Milly discover the mystery of Manor Hall?

The Girl with Green Eyes

JOHN ESCOTT

Greg is a porter at the Shepton Hotel in New York.

When a girl with beautiful green eyes asks him for help, Greg can't say no.

The girl's name is Cassie, and she says she is an artist. She tells Greg that her stepfather has her sketchbooks, and now she wants them back.

Cassie also says her stepfather is staying at Greg's hotel . . . so what could go wrong?

Taxi of Terror

PHILLIP BURROWS AND MARK FOSTER

'How does it work?' Jack asks when he opens his present – a mobile phone. Later that night, Jack is a prisoner in a taxi in the empty streets of the dark city. He now tries his mobile phone for the first time. Can it save his life?